Open the Quik
Ange

A KNOCK AT THE DOOR

This book is dedicated to dreamers everywhere. And to Tink, for repairing my wings. – A.S.

WHEN WAS THE

last time you...

HAD A

conversation

WITH THE moon?

OR MADE A wish

ON A

falling star?

HELD HOPE
from a string

of delicate things?

WHEN WAS THE

last time you...

got lost

OR WERE KISSED
by a prince

WHO TURNED

into a frog?

CONSULTED
a caterpillar

OR KIDNAPPED
a myth?

WHEN WAS THE

last time you...

had a visit

FROM YOUR
faery godmother

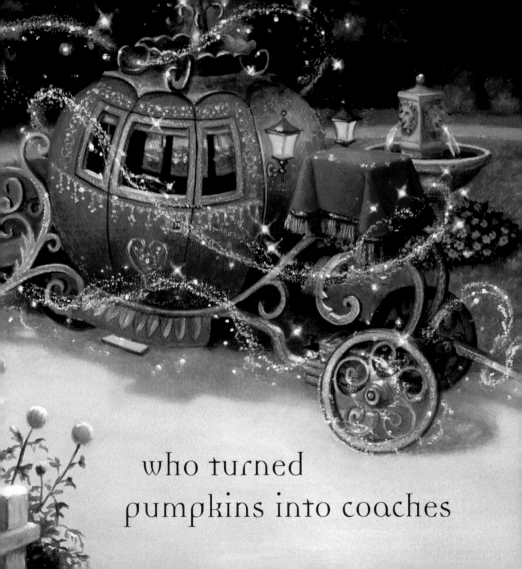

who turned
pumpkins into coaches

and wishes

into wings?

WHEN WAS THE

last time you...

CRIED lost tears

INTO THE
lake of longing?

sipped inspiration

FROM THE
pool of wonder?

OR ROSE, victorious,

LIKE A phoenix

FROM THE ashes?

WHEN DID

you last...

LAY YOUR HEAD

in the lap of awe

AND LISTEN TO A
song

FROM A

distant shore

CALLED home?

THE TIME IS

now

leap!

soar

explore...

REMEMBER
your dreams

and unseen things

sing with rapture

and dance...

dance...

dance like a dervish!

AND WHEN

inspiration knocks

open the door!

Concept, text and editing:
ANGI SULLINS

Graphic design:
SILAS TOBALL

Published by Amber Lotus Publishing
PO Box 11329, Portland, Oregon 97211
800.326.2375 • www.amberlotus.com

Second printing: 2008
10 9 8 7 6 5 4 3 2

Printed in China

Licensed by
Duirwaigh, Inc.
PO Box 441071
Kennesaw, Georgia 30144
info@Duirwaigh.com
www.Duirwaigh.com

Music: Martine Lund Hoel
Hardanger fiddle and flutes,
Bent Bredeveien: Synth and guitars,
Kenneth Aspeslåen: Drums and percussion.
Composed by Martine Lund Hoel, arranged
by Bent Bredeveien and Kenneth Aspeslåen.
Produced and mixed by Bent Bredeveien.
www.hardingfiddler.com.
Copyright Protected – All Rights Reserved
Martine Lund Hoel.

Amber Lotus Publishing edition ISBN: 978-1-60237-120-0

CREDITS & COPYRIGHTS

Artwork by:

Veronica Atanacio	www.folkvangar.com
Pat Brennan	www.moonmomma.co.uk
Ian Daniels	www.DuirwaighGallery.com
Jena DellaGrottaglia-Maldonado	www.autumnsgoddess.deviantart.com
Angel Dominguez	www.DuirwaighGallery.com
Marc Fishman	www.MarkFishman.com
Barry Greenland	www.bazzabent.deviantart.com
Gary Lippincott	www.GaryLippincott.com
Susan McKivergan	www.cosmosue.net
Michael Orwick	www.MichaelOrwick.com
Marc Potts	www.MarcPotts.com
Ruth Sanderson	www.RuthSanderson.com
Greg Spalenka	www.Spalenka.com
Matt Stewart	www.DuirwaighGallery.com
Silas Toball	www.SilasToball.com
Christophe Vacher	www.Vacher.com

I sat down during the first
windy weeks of November 2004
to contemplate Christmas gifts for the
Duirwaigh artists. I am often referred to
as the Muse of Duirwaigh Gallery, but I
must confess my ability to inspire would
dry up completely if it weren't for the
artists I know. It was important to me, with
Christmas coming, to convey to them their
significance and thank them for the dreams
and visions they had brought to my life.

That is how *A Knock at the Door* began,
as a Thank You to the artists who inspire me.

We posted the film to our website, and within days it was
circulating worldwide. Our daily web visits exploded

and letters poured in from men, women, and children from all corners of the world. Some were in hospitals, some at their offices, some wrote to us in the middle of the night with tears pouring down their cheeks. But they all shared one thing: Hope.

Whether your dream is to heal or to help, to create or to compose, to dance, paint, sing, or—most importantly—to live more joyfully, the magic is inside you.

I have a theory: The reason *A Knock at the Door* has made such an impact on people's lives is because it causes people to **remember**. When we see or hear something inspirational, it is like holding a mirror to our souls. It helps remind us the magic is inside. We owned and used it in childhood and somehow lost it along the arduous road to adulthood.

No matter how far you've traveled from your center, you can always return to it. Inspiration IS. It waits. It stands outside the door of your Imagination, hoping you'll hear its patient call.

Knock. Knock. Knock.

All you have to do is open.

Brightly Woven,
Angi

Between the worlds of right and wrong
Inside the Duirwaigh wood,
We beckon weary passers-by
"Forsake the world of 'should'!"

Rekindle long lost hopes and dreams
Refuse the ordinary
Engage your heart in matters light
Entice Extraordinary

Remember how to love unleashed
Remember why you're here!
Not just today or holidays
Remember through the year!

www.DuirwaighGallery.com
an oasis for the travel-weary soul seeking inspiration
in an all-too mundane world.